SMDS
HOLLINSWOOD JUNIORS

SMDS
MADELEY COURT SCHOOL
COURT STREET, MADELEY
TELFORD TF7 5DZ
Telephone: 585704

E.M.E.S.
WALKER HOUSE
RADBROOK COLLEGE
RADBROOK ROAD
SHREWSBURY
SY3 9BJ

SMDS
MADELEY COURT SCHOOL
COURT STREET, MADELEY
TELFORD TF7 5DZ
Telephone: 585704

France is my country

In this book 28 people from all over France tell you what their life is like - life in the factory, life on the farm, and life in the big cities.

FRANCE
is my country

Bernice and Cliff Moon

My Country

America is my country
Australia is my country
Britain is my country
China is my country
Denmark is my country
France is my country
Greece is my country
India is my country
Israel is my country
Italy is my country
Kenya is my country
New Zealand is my country
Spain is my country

Further titles are in preparation

This book is based on an original text and photographs by James Tomlins

First published in 1983 by
Wayland (Publishers) Limited
61 Western Road, Hove
East Sussex BN3 1JD, England

© Copyright 1983 Wayland (Publishers) Limited

Second impression 1985

Third impression 1986

ISBN 0 85078 320 8

Phototypeset by VDU Characters Ltd., Burgess Hill
Sussex, England
Printed in Italy by G. Canale & C. S.p.A., Turin

Contents

Arianne, *schoolgirl*   6
Georges, *taxi driver*   8
Jean, *priest*   10
Emile, *bistro owner*   12
Gerard, *hotel worker*   14
Robert, *dentist*   16
Soraya, *unemployed*   18
Gerard, *police inspector*   20
Jack and Andrée, *bakers*   22
Jean-Pierre, *teacher*   24
Solange, *telex operator*   26
Georges, *chef*   28
Monique, *shopkeeper (gifts)*   30
Jean-Pierre, *journalist*   32
Ghislaine, *secretary*   34
Auguste, *cobbler*   36
Alfred, *scientist*   38
Roger, *pig farmer*   40
Claude, *trade union leader*   42
Charlette, *shopkeeper (perfume)*   44
Elizabeth, *housewife*   46
Jean-Christophe, *student*   48
Jacques, *factory manager*   50
Jean, *expert on Eskimos*   52
Odile, *nurse*   54
Julien, *artist*   56
Jean, *mayor*   58
Claude, *bank manager*   60
Facts   62
Index   64

I am Arianne and I am a schoolgirl.

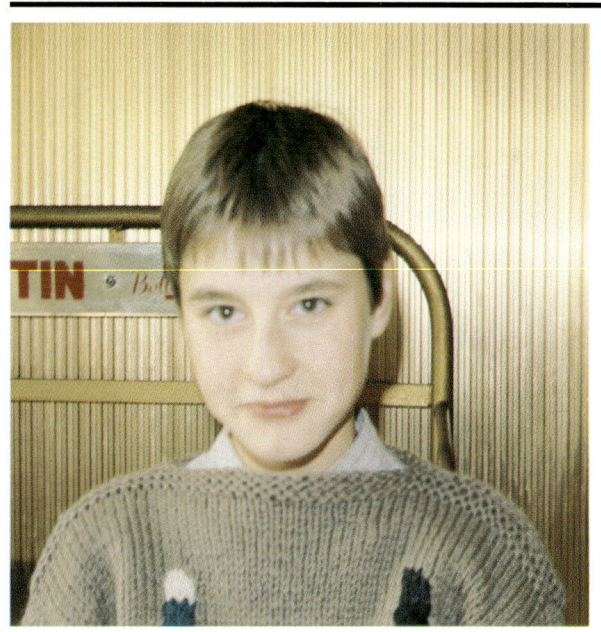

I go to a secondary school in Orléans.
There are 500 boys and girls at our school.
We don't have a school uniform but
the teachers are very strict about everything else.
We start school early in the morning at 8.00 a.m. and
we don't finish until 4.30 p.m.

This is my class at school. ➡

Not long ago French children
had to buy their own
books, pens and pencils.
This girl is finding the books
she needed for school.
Now everything is free at school.

I live quite near my school and I go on my bike.
My favourite lessons are English and maths.
We also have art, French and German lessons.
We have three hours of sport every week and
I like playing handball and volleyball best.
You can have swimming lessons if you want to.
I think I work very hard at school but
my reports always say I talk too much!

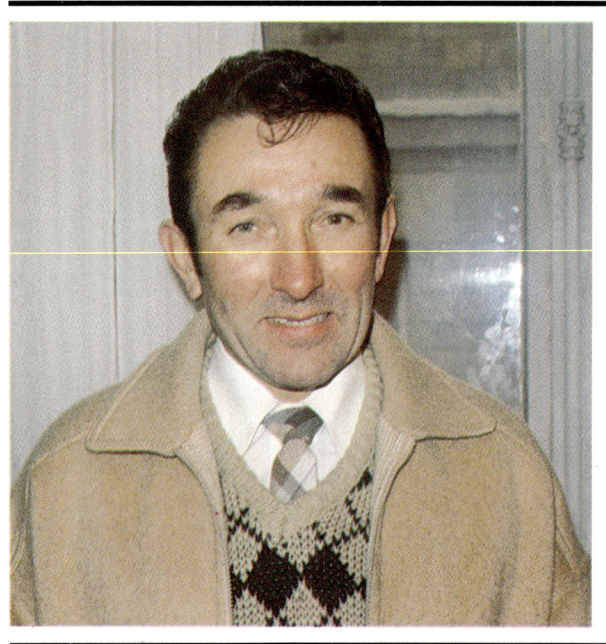

I am Georges and I drive a taxi.

Can you find Paris on the map at the front of this book?
That is where I drive my taxi.
My day starts at 6.00 a.m. and ends at 7.00 p.m.
I take an hour off to go home for my lunch.
There are lots of taxi drivers like me in Paris —
in fact there are 14,500 of us!

I have been a taxi driver in Paris for 18 years.

I own my taxi but some taxi drivers work for big companies.
They have radios to help them. A radio would drive *me* mad!
When people want a taxi they stop me in the street.
I have about 14 to 18 customers a day.
All taxi drivers who own their own taxis
are finding it more and more difficult
to pay for petrol and other running costs.
I have to work a longer and longer day to make enough money!
In a few years I shall retire and grow roses.
I have a small garden where I grow my roses and
I think about them all day as I drive around Paris.

This is the rush hour
in Paris.
I have to drive
very carefully when
it is like this.

My name is Jean and I am a priest.

This is the church where I work.
Three other priests help me.
I wanted to be a priest
when I was 7 years old.
I spent five years in Rome
before I became a priest.
Most of the time
I work with young people.
We have a scout troop and
we often have talks and outings.

This is a cathedral in Paris.
It is called *Notre Dame,*
which means 'Our Lady'.
Many people come to see
Notre Dame because it is
very beautiful.
As you can see, my church
is much smaller
than Notre Dame.

Another job we have to do is look after tramps.
They need food, clothes and money.
Sometimes it is hard to help them because
we are so short of money ourselves.
There are many problems if you are a priest
working in a big city but it is the only job I want to do.

My name is Emile and I own a bistro.

This is my café. It is called a bistro in France.
If you come to my bistro you can sit at a table
on the pavement or you can sit inside if it is cold.
I make very good cups of coffee and I also sell a lot of red wine.
Many of my customers buy water and
some of the water they drink is fizzy.

This is a much larger French café.
More and more people are going to big cafés like this one instead of going to bistros.

Are you hungry?
I cook very good sausage and chips and
toasted ham-and-cheese sandwiches.
You can sit in my bistro for as long as you like.
I am open six days a week from 6.00 a.m. until about 9.00 p.m.
In France you can buy and drink wine at any time.
I close my bistro when the last customer goes!
I work 15 hours a day, running from customer to customer.
I haven't spent one day ill in bed for the last 20 years.
I haven't time to be ill!

I am Gerard and I work in a hotel.

A lot of the people who stay in our hotel go to see this church. It is called *Sacre Coeur* which means 'Sacred Heart' in English.
It stands on a hill and you can see it from a long way away.

This is the Eiffel Tower.
I should think that
everyone who comes to Paris
goes to see it.
You can go up the Tower
in a lift.
The view from the top
is wonderful.

I started hotel work when I was 17 years old.
First I was a student for three years.
Next I worked in a hotel kitchen but
it was hard work washing all the pots and pans.
Then I helped a chef for a while.
After the kitchens, I worked in the restaurant and then
I worked in the wine cellar.
My job now is in the office at the hotel entrance.
I look after the visitors when they arrive and
I make sure they are comfortable and get whatever they need.

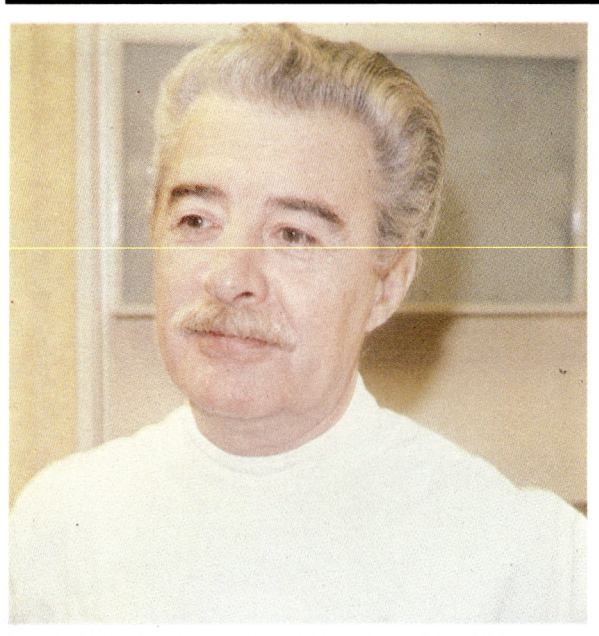

My name is Robert and I am a dentist.

Yes, I am a dentist!
Like all dentists, I say to my patients,
'You must use your toothbrush twice a day.'

Here are some posters
which tell my patients
how they can look after
their teeth.
Can you find the poster that
tells you about toothbrushes?

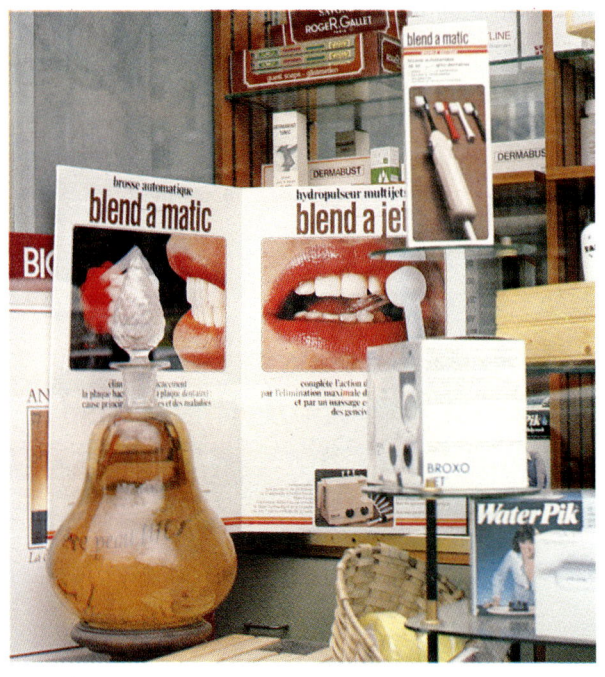

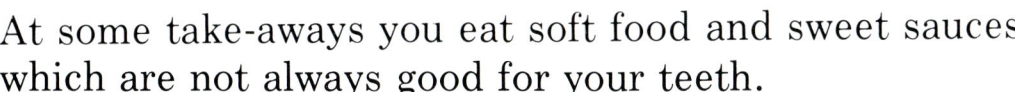

At some take-aways you eat soft food and sweet sauces which are not always good for your teeth.

Of course, if you eat plenty of fresh food and
not too much sugar, your teeth will stay healthy
for a long time.
What you eat makes all the difference to your teeth.
Young people keep us very busy because
they like to eat and drink sweet things.
We have adverts on television to tell them
how to look after their teeth.
Some dentists go to schools to check children's teeth.
My best patients come for a check-up every six months
and they brush their teeth twice a day.

I am Soraya and I can't get a job.

I am 18 years old and I left school six months ago.
In France many young people find it hard to get a job.

The people at the job centres are very helpful.
They tell us about jobs that may interest us.

These are foreign students.
It is even harder
to get a job if you come
from another country.

I read about four newspapers every day
to see if there are any jobs.
I have even put an advert in a newspaper myself.
Last week I missed a job by a few minutes.
My bus was late and another girl got there before me.
I have been to England twice to work but those jobs
were only for a short time.
At the moment I am trying to get a job in a shop.
If I get a job I shall save my money
so that I can go to an acting school.
I dream about working in a theatre one day.

My name is Gerard and I am a police inspector.

I have worked for the police for 24 years.
You may think that the police only catch criminals but really they have several jobs to do.
In the picture you can see a policeman controlling traffic.
That is just one of the things we have to do.

◀ This is the building where robbers are tried.

When very important people visit Paris
a special police unit looks after them.
There is also a special unit for controlling crowds.
There are five burglaries an hour in Paris and
of course the robbers have to be caught.
I don't like it when they have guns.
A man rushed at me once with an axe.
I was very frightened but I managed to catch him.
People don't feel safe in the streets of Paris at night but
we are trying to make things better for them.
Some people think that all the police in France
are called *gendarmes* but that is not so.
Gendarmes are like soldiers and they live in barracks.

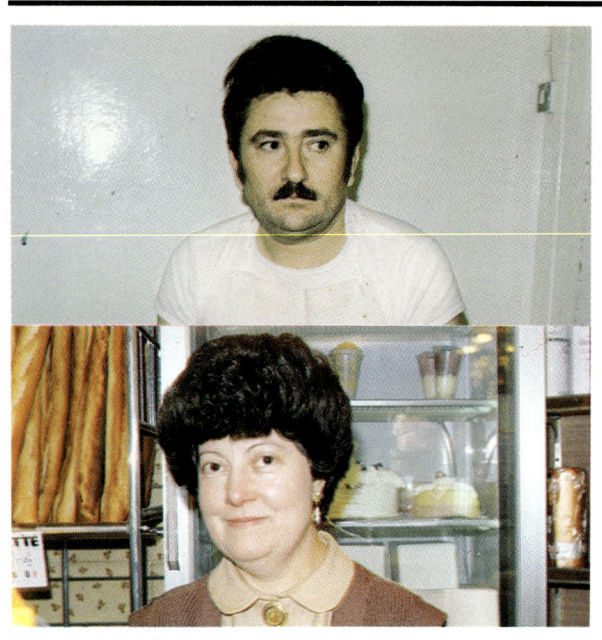

Our names are Jack and Andree. We are bakers.

This is our shop.
Can you see the long loaves?
They are very fresh and crusty.
We use the best white flour.
We start work at 4.00 a.m.
There are seven of us
working in the bakery and
serving in the shop.
Sometimes we serve
1,000 customers a day.
We also bake bread
for a large school
and three bistros.

Can you see how many loaves this man has bought at our shop?
You can buy French bread in 19 different shapes and
we make them all by hand.

French bread goes stale very quickly but
we bake it fresh *every* day.
At Christmas we make chocolate Father Christmas shapes and
at Easter we make chocolate rabbits and fishes.
They are very expensive and we don't sell many.
We don't mind though because we enjoy making them and
they make the shop window look cheerful.

I am Jean-Pierre.
I am a teacher.

This is my school.
It doesn't look very big from the outside but when you go inside it is as big as a village!
There are 1,450 children at the school who are from 4 to 16 years old.
There are 100 teachers.
As for me, I have taught here for 32 years!

Here I am in my study.
When I am not teaching I am very busy
getting lessons ready for the next day.

The children at my school cannot have games
because we only have a very small playground.
It would be nice to take the children
to a large playing field.
But I mustn't grumble, the older children
get very good marks in exams at this school.
In fact, they are usually the best marks in France!

I am Solange and I send telex messages.

A telex is like a telephone call except the message is written, not spoken.
The machine which does this is called a teleprinter.
When I started this job in 1962 there were only two of us who were telex operators.
Now, nearly every message sent overseas goes by telex.

This is a new transmitter for sending telex messages.

Look at these modern
telephone kiosks.
They are made of glass.
you can dial a call
to anywhere in the world
from some of them.

I start work at 7.00 p.m. and finish at midnight.
In one evening I make calls all over the world.
Many of the calls are for newspapers.
I have to make sure the message is correct and
I always check every word very carefully.
A message can be in any language so I have learnt
to read English, German, Spanish and Italian.
We are a telex family — my husband is a telex worker
and our son is training to do the same work as us!

I am Georges and I am a chef.

You may think that a chef only cooks but, in fact, a chef has many jobs to do.

Look at the picture of the butcher's shop.
It is near my restaurant and I go there every day to choose the best meat for my cooking.

These cleaners are getting
my restaurant ready
for our first customers.

One of my important jobs is choosing good wine.
I go where the wine is made and taste it myself.
I only sell the best wine in my restaurant.
By the time I have done all the shopping
it is time to start cooking.
What is on the menu today?
A casserole of snails, a thick slice of duck's breast
with mushroom sauce and then apple pudding.
How would you like that for your dinner?
Our first customers are here!
I show them to their table and then help them choose
what they would like to eat and drink.
My father and grandfather were chefs so there isn't much
I don't know about running a restaurant.

I am Monique and I have a gift shop.

Yes, I sell gifts for adults and toys for children.
Lots of French children come to my shop and of course,
their parents come to buy Christmas and birthday presents.

Do you think these children
came to my shop
to buy their buckets?
Perhaps I sold
the climbing frame too!

30

This is what you would see if you came into my little shop.
Would you like a silver windmill, a key ring
or perhaps you need a birthday card?

My shop is very tiny but there are lots of things
on the shelves.
Christmas is a very busy time for me.
I sell electronic games, puzzles, watches and calculators.
I don't seem to sell as many Christmas cards as I used to.
Maybe people are using the telephone instead.
This shop belonged to my grandfather and he gave it to me.
I was born here so I know everyone.
I can usually guess which toy my customers will choose!

I am Jean-Pierre.
I am a journalist.

If you write for newspapers you are called a *journalist*.
I have been a journalist for several years.

Here are some of the newspapers and magazines
which you can buy in France.
As you can see, there are a lot to choose from.

This old lady enjoys reading her newspaper.
She will sit in the sun and read about what is happening in France and other places.

First a journalist has to find his news and then
the story has to be written or reported.
I have even been to other countries to report on their news.
I enjoy that because I like travelling.
I am also writing a book in my spare time and
I hope it will be good enough to be published.
When I was young I never thought that
I would end up as a journalist.
In fact, I wanted to be a teacher!

I am Ghislaine.
I am a secretary.

Can you find Marseilles on the map of France?
That is where I have worked as a secretary for eight years.
Marseilles is in the south of France and
it can be very hot in summer.

I don't work on Saturdays
and Sundays.
I love to go out with
my family at weekends.

You may think that a secretary has to type letters all day
but nowadays secretaries have all kinds of jobs to do.
We have to learn to use modern office machines
like the one in the picture.

When I started work eight years ago
my office was very small.
It was badly lit and rather uncomfortable.
Today, offices are very pleasant places.
We have modern desks and comfortable chairs.
The lighting is better and we even have pictures
on the walls and plants in window boxes.

I am Auguste and I mend shoes.

What does this shop sell?
You can buy lovely new shoes here but one day
those shoes will need mending.
Not many shoes are made from leather these days.
If a customer brings me some leather shoes to mend
my eyes light up and I can't wait to get started.
Why? Because that's what I like best —
mending a pair of real leather shoes!

Leather is very expensive but I love cutting and
shaping it with my tools.
I can make your worn-out shoes look like new.
How many customers do you think I get in one day?
Usually I see about a hundred so I am kept very busy.
In winter I have to work very hard.
Everyone is in a hurry, so soles and heels
must be mended as quickly as possible.
I can put a small heel on a woman's shoe
in just one minute.
That's how skilled I am!

Here I am in my shop
mending a shoe.
The shoe is upside-down
on a cobbler's *last*.

I am Alfred and I am a scientist.

This is a very famous school where scientists are trained in Paris.
When I was 14 years old, my teachers noticed that I was very good at maths.
That helped me to get a place at this famous school.
I was very lucky to be a student here.

These special machines
will be used in
a nuclear power station.
What I have found out
about atoms will help
other scientists who work
in nuclear power stations.

After my training I became a teacher for several years.
Then I started finding out all I could about atoms.
I had ten people to help me.
After a lot of hard work we found out
something *new* about atoms.
There is a special prize for scientists who find out new things.
It is called the Nobel Prize and only a few scientists win it.
My work made me famous and I won the Nobel Prize!

My name is Roger.
I have a pig farm.

I have about 1,000 pigs on my farm.
I give them plenty to eat to make them fat
so that I can sell them to the pork butcher.
French people like pork so much that
we can't fatten enough pigs ourselves.
We have to buy pork from other countries as well.

Here are some of my pigs.

There are lots of special shops
like this all over France
where you can buy cold meats.
These shops sell a lot of pork.

I have lived on the pig farm all my life.
I was born here and my father was the farmer here too.
Now *my* son helps *me* so you can see
we are a family of farmers.
My son and I work about ten hours a day and
my wife works about three hours a day on the farm as well.
As well as looking after our pigs
we grow some of the food that they eat.
Our pigs eat a lot of maize and barley.
We also have about 20 cows and they have to be looked after.
We would never have time to go on holiday!

My name is Claude and I am a trade union leader.

Can you find Limoges on the map of France?
Limoges is well-known for its factories.
Limoges is my home and it was here
that I first heard about trade unions.

This is the main office of one of the biggest trade unions in France.

This is a big meeting of trade unionists and
it is called a *mass rally.*
The banners say what the workers are asking for.

Trade unions try to make sure that workers get good wages
and safe places to work.
If the workers in my union are unhappy about something
I go to see the factory owner to sort out the problem.
Sometimes that doesn't work and then all the workers
have a big meeting like the one in the picture.
I have done a lot for the workers in my union.
They have longer holidays and better pensions when they retire.
Also they get a year's pay if they lose their jobs.
In fact, we were the first union in the world
to get that for our members.

I am Charlette and I sell perfume.

Look for Nice on the map of France.
Nice is in the south of France and that is where
I have a perfume shop.

Here you can see where some of my perfumes are made.

Perfume must smell pleasant and
the smell must last a long time.
In this picture the perfume maker
is testing the smell of his perfumes.
He has to do it carefully because the perfume
will be very expensive and a lot of it
will be sold in other countries.

I have had my shop for three years.
For the first few weeks I didn't have a single customer!
Now I have about 25 customers a day.
I like having the smell of perfumes around me all day.
It seems to stop me from feeling tired!

I am Elizabeth and I am a housewife.

Can you find Rennes on the map of France?
That is where I live with my husband and
our three children.

I like to shop in a market
like this.
The fruit and vegetables
are very fresh and
they don't cost too much!

Sometimes I go shopping at a very large supermarket like this.
It is called a hypermarket.
I go there for coffee, drinking chocolate, jam,
cheese, fish and meat.
I don't buy lamb because it is too expensive.

I am always the first to get up in the mornings.
I help my two older children to get ready for school.
I also have Jennifer, my baby, to look after.
Every day there is washing, ironing and shopping to do.
My children come home from school for their lunch and
they are always hungry!
Our favourite meal is Sunday lunch because
that is the only time the whole family sits down
together for a meal.

My name is Jean-Christophe. I am a student.

Nowadays it costs a lot to be a student.
My friends play in a band to earn some extra money.
They play on a busy street outside the shops and
if the shoppers like the music they put money in the boxes.
Then my friends share out the money to buy books,
clothes and food.

Here are my friends playing in their band.

Students can sit outside
a bistro for as long
as they like. ▶
They meet their friends,
talk and even write.

I study how people used to live a long, long time ago.
This is called the study of *archaeology.*
At the moment I am studying how people found out about fire.
There was no electricity in those days and
before they had fire their food was always cold and
they couldn't keep themselves warm.
Nowadays you only have to switch on the electricity
to get a hot dinner or a warm bedroom!
How do archaeologists find out how people used to live?
One way is to dig up the soil and collect the things they find.
So if you would like to be an archaeologist
you must be able to draw what you find and, of course,
you must be good at digging!

I am Jacques and I am a factory manager.

Can you guess what this shop sells?
Look at the big green cross over the door.
It is a chemist's shop and French people
buy their medicines there.
My factory makes a lot of the pills and medicines
that you can buy in a chemist's shop.

➡

This is what the inside
of my factory looks like.
The machines have lots
of tubes, switches and lights.

A manager of a busy factory has many jobs to do.
To start with, there are 250 men and women
working in my factory.
I help them to be very careful with their work.
The factory must keep up-to-date
with new ways of making medicines.
It is good to know that what we make can save people's lives.
I work very long hours but I *do* get some time off and then
I like to play volleyball or tennis.
It is important to keep fit if you are a manager.

I am Jean and I am an expert on Eskimos.

I am a scientist and I study how people live
in different parts of the world.
I am very interested in Eskimos.
I have just made a film about Eskimos for French television.
I used three teams of men to help me with the filming and
it has taken two years to finish the film.

This is near the North Pole
where we made our film.
Up here you need lots
of warm clothes
to stay alive.

This is a picture of an Eskimo that I took in Canada.
The Eskimo is using dogs to pull his sledge.

I feel sad when I think about how Eskimos live now.
Only a few of them build igloos or use dogs.
We had a big meeting in Rouen to talk about Eskimos.
Lots of other scientists wanted to help them.
I love the land of ice and snow where Eskimos live.
When I die, I want to be buried there!

I am Odile and I am a nurse.

French doctors like using injections to make people better.
The doctor sends patients to me for their injections.
Many of my patients need injections every day
for weeks or even months.

Here are two of my patients.
I see about 30 or 40 patients
like these every day.
I have to visit
a lot of them
in their own homes.

The ambulance is coming out of a very modern hospital called the *Bichat* in Paris.

I work a 12-hour day starting at 8.00 a.m.
I must also be ready for emergencies and
sometimes I have to work on Sundays.
My patients are often old people but I also see babies.
One of my patients is 100 years old!
I don't wear a uniform like nurses in England, but sometimes
I think it would be nice to have a uniform
like an English nurse!

I am Julien and I am an artist.

Paris is well-known for its beautiful paintings and many artists come to live here.
I suppose I am a very lucky artist because I have my own gallery in Paris.
My gallery is not as big as the Beaubourg Centre near Notre Dame Cathedral.

This is the Beaubourg Centre.
Some of the best paintings in the world are here.

In Paris you will find artists painting pictures
all the year round.

Many of the artists paint pictures of famous buildings
so that tourists will buy them to take home as presents.
Three different kinds of people come to my gallery
to buy paintings.
Some people collect paintings just like collecting stamps.
Some buy paintings because they are valuable and
some buy a painting just because they like it.
My mother is also a painter but she lives in the south of France.
I suppose I was born to be an artist!

My name is Jean and I am the Mayor of Poissy.

If you find Poissy on the map of France you will see that it is a small town which is very near Paris. Poissy has a large car factory and, of course, a lot of factory workers live in the town.

This is the car factory at Poissy.

One of the things I have to do is to help workers
who lose their jobs at the car factory.
I can even give them money if they are really in trouble.
The car workers like to live near the factory
so we are always short of houses in Poissy.
I have set up projects to build comfortable houses
with cheap rents but this is not easy.
I have to borrow a lot of money from the bank
to pay for the new houses.
I also have to make sure the schools' buildings and equipment
are kept in good condition.
A mayor like me has to lead his town.

This road needs mending.
A mayor in France
makes sure the roads
are kept in good order.

My name is Claude and I am a bank manager.

Do you have pocket money each week?
If you come to my bank in Paris I will look after it for you until you need it!
Most of the people I help have small businesses.
Fifteen years ago not many people had a bank account but now almost everybody has a cheque book.

This where French gold is kept safe.
Sometimes there is £2,600,000,000 worth of gold in this building!

60

Some banks are very beautiful.
This room belongs to the Bank of France and
important bank meetings are held here.

Many new banks have been opened in France in recent years.
France has four of the biggest banks in the world.
There is an old French saying, 'As safe as a bank'.
But that is probably not true today because
three gunmen attacked us in our bank 18 months ago.
I was terrified but luckily I wasn't hurt.
The danger doesn't worry me too much.
People come to me with their money problems.
They always go out of my office looking much happier.
Yes, I am glad I became a bank manager because
it gives me a chance to help people.

Facts

Capital City The capital city of France is called Paris.

Language Most people in France speak French.
A few people in Brittany speak Breton and
a few people in the south west speak Basque.

Money French people pay for things
with francs and centimes.
There are 100 centimes in 1 franc.

Religion Most people in France are Roman Catholics.

Weather In the south of France
it can be very hot in summer,
but in the north the weather is the same
as in Britain. In the rest of France it is usually
warmer and drier than in Britain.

Government France doesn't have a king or queen.
Instead the French people elect a President.
The President chooses a Prime Minister and
other government ministers.
A new President is elected every 7 years.

Houses A third of the houses in France
are over 100 years old.
A lot of modern houses and flats have been built
in the last 30 years.

Schools   French children start school
when they are six years old.
They go to Primary and Secondary Schools.
The school leaving age is 16.
There are 62 universities, 6 university centres
and 3 polytechnics in France.

Farming   The farms in France mainly grow wheat,
sugar-beet and barley. They also grow sunflowers
for oil and, of course, vines to make wine.
The farms grow almost enough to meet
the country's needs - France does not have to buy
much food from other countries.

Factories   Factories in France make food, clothes,
chemicals, building materials, engines, cars and
machines.

News   There are more than 100 daily
newspapers in France.
There are 7 broadcasting companies with 3 TV
channels and 4 radio stations.
There are also 21 local radio stations.

Index

archaeology 49
artists 56, 57

bakers 22, 23
banks 59, 60, 61
bistros 12, 13, 22, 49

cafés 12, 13, 22, 49
chefs 15, 28, 29
churches 10, 11, 14
cobblers 36, 37
crime 20, 21, 61

dentists 16, 17

Eiffel Tower 15

factories 50, 51, 58, 59, 62
farming 40, 41, 62
food 12, 13, 17, 22, 23, 28, 29, 40, 41, 46, 47

gifts 30, 31
government 62

houses 59, 62
hotels 14, 15

journalists 32, 33

languages 7, 27, 62
Limoges 42

Marseilles 34
mayors 58, 59
medicine 50, 51, 54, 55

newspapers 19, 27, 32, 33, 62
Nice 44
Nobel Prize 39
nursing 54, 55

offices 34, 35
Orléans 6

Paris 8, 9, 11, 14, 15, 21, 38, 56, 57, 62
perfume 44, 45
pigs 40, 41
Poissy 58, 59
police 20, 21
priests 10, 11

radio 9, 62
religion 10, 11, 62
Rennes 46
restaurants 15, 28, 29

schools 6, 7, 22, 24, 25, 38, 47, 59, 62
scientists 38, 39
secretaries 34, 35
shoes 36, 37
shops 22, 23, 28, 30, 31, 36, 41, 44, 46, 47, 48, 50
sport 7, 25
students 48, 49

taxis 8, 9
teachers 6, 24, 25, 39
telephones 27, 31
television 17, 52, 62

telex 26, 27
tourists 14, 15, 57
toys 30, 31
trade unions 42, 43

unemployment 18, 19

weather 34, 62
wine 12, 13, 29, 62